10422182

Horses

American Quarter

Horses

by Kim O'Brien

Consulting Editor: Gail Saunders-Smith, PhD

Capstone press®

Mankato, Minnesota

Pebble Books are published by Capstone Press,
151 Good Counsel Drive, P.O. Box 669, Mankato, Minnesota 56002.
www.capstonepress.com

1 2 3 4 5 6 14 13 12 11 10 09

Library of Congress Cataloging-in-Publication Data
O'Brien, Kim.
    American quarter horses / by Kim O'Brien.
    p. cm. — (Pebble books. Horses)
    Includes bibliographical references and index.
    Summary: "A brief introduction to the characteristics, life cycle, and uses of
the American quarter horse breed" — Provided by publisher.
    ISBN-13: 978-1-4296-2232-5 (hardcover)
    ISBN-10: 1-4296-2232-6 (hardcover)
    1. Quarter horse — Juvenile literature. I. Title.
SF293.Q3O27 2009
636.1'33 — dc22   2008026825

Note to Parents and Teachers

The Horses set supports national science standards related to
life science. This book describes and illustrates American quarter
horses. The images support early readers in understanding the
text. The repetition of words and phrases helps early readers learn
new words. This book also introduces early readers to subject
specific vocabulary words, which are defined in the Glossary
section. Early readers may need assistance to read some words and
to use the Table of Contents, Glossary, Read More, Internet Sites,
and Index sections of the book.

Table of Contents

A Sprinting Horse 5
From Foal to Adult 11
Riding and Rodeos 15

Glossary 22
Read More 23
Internet Sites. 23
Index 24

4

A Sprinting Horse

The American quarter horse
is a fast sprinter.
It runs faster
than other horse breeds
over a short distance.

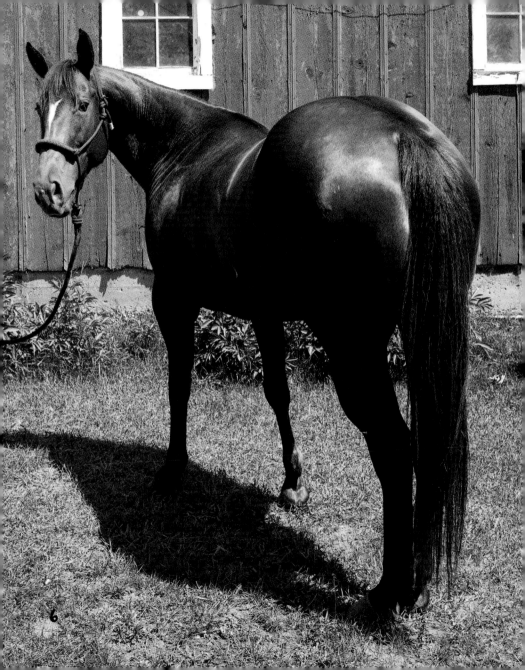

6

Quarter horses have muscular bodies. Strong hindquarters give the horses quick bursts of speed.

sorrel

dun

8

Quarter horses' coats
can be one of many colors.
Sorrel, dun, and gray
are common coat colors.

From Foal to Adult

Female quarter horses give birth to one foal at a time. Newborn foals have fuzzy coats and wobbly legs.

Quarter horses are
fully grown after
about four years.
Adults stand
14.2 to 16 hands high.

Horses are measured in hands.
Each hand is 4 inches (10 centimeters).
A horse is measured from the ground
to its withers.

Riding and Rodeos

Quarter horses are calm. People like riding them on trails.

Quarter horses help
ranch workers herd cattle.
The horses can stop
and start quickly
to follow the moving cattle.

People ride quarter horses
in rodeos.
These quick horses race
around barrels.

Quarter horses are gentle and hardworking.
They are popular horses for all kinds of riders.

Glossary

breed — a certain kind of animal within an animal group

dun — a brown coat color with a dark stripe of hair along the back and darker hair on the legs

foal — a young horse or pony

herd — to round up animals, such as cattle, and keep them together

hindquarter — the part of a horse where the back leg and rump connect to the body

muscular — having strong muscles

rodeo — a contest in which people ride horses and bulls, rope cattle, and race around barrels

sorrel — a light red body color with a lighter mane and tail color

sprinter — a horse that runs very quickly over short distances

Read More

Dell, Pamela. *American Quarter Horses.* Majestic Horses. Chanhassen, Minn.: Child's World, 2007.

Pitts, Zachary. *The Pebble First Guide to Horses.* Pebble First Guides. Mankato, Minn.: Capstone Press, 2009.

Internet Sites

FactHound offers a safe, fun way to find educator-approved Internet sites related to this book.

Here's what you do:
1. Visit *www.facthound.com*
2. Choose your grade level.
3. Begin your search.

This book's ID number is 9781429622325.

FactHound will fetch the best sites for you!

Index

breeds, 5
calm, 15
cattle, 17
coats, 9, 11
foals, 11
gentle, 21
hands, 13
hardworking, 21
height, 13

herding, 17
hindquarters, 7
legs, 11
riding, 15, 19
rodeos, 19
speed, 5, 7, 19
sprinting, 5
trails, 15
withers, 13

Word Count: 141
Grade: 1
Early-Intervention Level: 16

Editorial Credits
Erika L. Shores, editor; Bobbi J. Wyss, designer;
    Sarah L. Schuette, photo shoot direction

Photo Credits
Capstone Press/Karon Dubke, 1, 8; TJ Thoraldson Digital Photography, cover, 4,
    6, 10, 12, 14, 16, 18, 20

The Capstone Press Photo Studio thanks Rick Brown, Abbey Viessman, Bob
Folsom, and Diane Fralish for their help with photo shoots.

Capstone Press thanks Robert Coleman, PhD, associate professor of
Equine Extension at the University of Kentucky, Lexington's Department
of Animal Sciences, for reviewing this book.

24